MW01601033

Wonder Full

Intimately Known, Abundantly Loved

An artistic invitation to Psalm 139

by Rachael Lofgren
Illustrated by Patti Lofgren

SINGING SPARROW PRESS

BEMIDJI, MINNESOTA

Scripture quotations marked (NIV) are taken from the Holy Bible, New International Version®, NIV®. Copyright © 1973, 1978, 1984, 2011 by Biblica, Inc.® Used by permission of Zondervan. All rights reserved worldwide. www.zondervan.com The "NIV" and "New International Version" are trademarks registered in the United States Patent and Trademark Office by Biblica, Inc.®

Scripture quotations marked (BSB) are taken from The Holy Bible, Berean Standard Bible, BSB. Copyright ©2016, 2020 by Bible Hub. Used by Permission. All Rights Reserved Worldwide.

Scripture quotations marked ESV® Bible are from the ESV®Bible (The Holy Bible, English Standard Version®), copyright©2001 by Crossway Bibles, a publishing ministry of Good News Publishers. Used by permission. All rights reserved.

Scripture quotations marked NLT are taken from the Holy Bible, New Living Translation, Copyright © 1996, 2004, 2015 by Tyndale House Foundation. Used by permission of Tyndale House Publishers, Inc., Carol Stream, Illinois 60188. All rights reserved.

Scripture quotations marked TPT are from The Passion Translation®. Copyright © 2017, 2018, 2020 by Passion & Fire Ministries, Inc. Used by permission. All rights reserved. ThePassionTranslation.com.

Wonder Full

Copyright © 2023 by Rachael Lofgren (art and text)
Published by Singing Sparrow Press
Bemidji, Minnesota 56601
www.singingsparrowpress.com

ISBN 979-8-9882973-0-7

Printed in the United States

Dedication

To the One we worship. We feel Your pleasure.

Contents

Dear Reader,

Welcome to this artistic exploration of Psalm 139. As you browse this book, we desire to invite you into a space of wonder and joy in seeing God's goodness toward you in your story. As you think about the bigger story of Scripture represented in this Psalm, we pray that you will encounter a God who intimately knows you in all of life. As you stop to observe His care for you, may you be reminded that our good Creator perfectly and abundantly loves you and longs to build a personal relationship with you through His Son, Jesus, and His indwelling Spirit. We pray it will encourage you to look to the future with hope, with all our brothers and sisters in the body of Christ to the ultimate climax of the story of Scripture, Christ's return. When he makes everything new, we will live with Him in person forever in a perfect world! Then, we will fully know as we are known and experience His love in its perfection. What a beautiful thing to look forward to!

May you know the wonder of His loving presence today and always,

The Artists

Psalm 139 (TPT)

Lord, you know everything there is to know about me.
You perceive every movement of my heart and soul,
and you understand my every thought
before it even enters my mind.

You are so intimately aware of me, Lord.
You read my heart like an open book
and you know all the words I'm about to speak
before I even start a sentence!
You know every step I will take before my journey even begins.

You've gone into my future to prepare the way,
and in kindness you follow behind me
to spare me from the harm of my past.
You have laid your hand on me!

This is just too wonderful, deep, and incomprehensible!
Your understanding of me brings me wonder and strength.

Where could I go from your Spirit?
Where could I run and hide from your face?

If I go up to heaven, you're there!
If I go down to the realm of the dead, you're there too!

If I fly with wings into the shining dawn, you're there!
If I fly into the radiant sunset, you're there waiting!

Wherever I go, your hand will guide me;
your strength will empower me.

It's impossible to disappear from you
or to ask the darkness to hide me,
for your presence is everywhere,
bringing light into my night.

There is no such thing as darkness with you.
The night, to you, is as bright as the day;
there's no difference between the two.

You formed my innermost being, shaping my delicate inside
and my intricate outside, and wove them all together in my mother's womb.

I thank you, God, for making me so mysteriously complex!
Everything you do is marvelously breathtaking.
It simply amazes me to think about it!
How thoroughly you know me, Lord!

You even formed every bone in my body
when you created me in the secret place;
carefully, skillfully you shaped me from nothing to something.

You saw who you created me to be before I became me!
Before I'd ever seen the light of day,
the number of days you planned for me
were already recorded in your book.

Every single moment you are thinking of me!

How precious and wonderful

to consider that you cherish me constantly in your every thought!
O God, your desires toward me are more
than the grains of sand on every shore!
When I awake each morning, you're still with me.

O God, come and slay these bloodthirsty, murderous men!
For I cry out, "Depart from me, you wicked ones!"

See how they blaspheme your sacred name
and lift up themselves against you, but all in vain!

Lord, can't you see how I despise those who despise you?
For I grieve when I see them rise up against you.

I have nothing but complete hatred and disgust for them.
Your enemies shall be my enemies!

God, I invite your searching gaze into my heart.
Examine me through and through;
find out everything that may be hidden within me.
Put me to the test and sift through all my anxious cares.

See if there is any path of pain I'm walking on,
and lead me back to your glorious, everlasting way—
the path that brings me back to you.

7

Fully Known

Oh God, who made the earth and sky,
The great expanse of all the sea;
With such great power, who am I?
That You see me?

You know me in my inward parts.
You know my thoughts from far away.
You wrote my life within your book;
You know each day.

You see my passions and my dreams,
When I awake and when I sleep;
You see me when I come and go,
And safely keep.

You saw me in my mother's womb,
Unborn, You knit my every part,
So fearfully and wonderfully,
Right from the start.

If I should wander far from home,
If I should try to hide from You,
I cannot, for your presence there,
Still sees through.

Oh God, by You so fully known,
And so unfathomably loved.
Help me to know You truly, too,
A Lover proved.

Created to be known.

**You have searched me, Lord,
and you know me.**

Psalm 139:1 (NIV)

I am a small town, lifelong friend sort of person. I have discovered this by moving a dozen times in as many years, living in cities with millions and villages with thousands. When I vacationed this year, I chose tiny towns with few people. Perhaps this could be chalked up to my being an introvert or growing up in a small-town setting. But no matter one's personality, if one would prefer the city, small-town living, group friendships, or individual, all humans naturally crave at least some relational contact with others. We seek some sort of spirituality or worship some form of knowledge or being beyond what we can see.

From the time we are born and our mother's voice soothes our first cries to the time we face the grave where we reach for the hands of loved ones as we are ushered into the unseen, we respond to and seek to know another. In art, romance, friendship, and even science, we constantly seek to know and ache to be known. Beyond it all is the invitation from a God who knows us intimately and created us in His image. The God who invites us to know Him, to seek and find Him as He pursues us, and finds us in all our earthly places.

You have searched me, Lord, and you know me.

Psalm 139:1 (NIV)

You know when I sit and when I rise...

Psalm 139:2a (NIV)

Table

You know when I sit and when I rise;
Psalm 139:2a (NIV)

God is generous and hospitable in how He knows us. He knows us not just when we converse with Him or as He seeks us when we wander from Him but in all our daily comings and goings. In Psalm 23, David talks about God's goodness and mercy following him. He says this immediately after painting a vivid picture of the table God prepares in the presence of his enemies providing an overflowing cup. Even in life's imperfections, when the moments we face are both frustrating and fulfilling, the lavish table He sets for us is filled with the thoughtful provision of His goodness.

All good and perfect gifts are from the Father. The daily grace of rhythms and schedules, meaningful work and play, nourishing food, and relationships. The things that make up our private lives, homes, and families, our little concerns and joys; He enters all of it. And in the challenging, painful times, He is there, too. He is there when life brings disappointment, sick children, flat tires, financial struggle, or weather that cancels plans. He knows our sitting and rising, our needs, and the things we think are too small for the One who runs the universe. Encouraging His followers about God's care in the details, Jesus said, "Are not two sparrows sold for a penny? Yet not one of them will fall to the ground outside your Father's care. And even the very hairs of your head are all numbered. So don't be afraid; you are worth more than many sparrows." Matthew 10:29-30 (NIV) God's care is so tenderly attentive that not a single detail escapes His notice. Nothing we face can take us outside His provision and protection. What a lavish table. What abundant love!

13

Longing

You perceive my thoughts from afar.
Psalm 139:2b (NIV)

We all have desires, things we dream of deep inside that we do not readily share with others. God sees and knows these thoughts, even when others do not. The Psalmist talks about God knowing his thoughts from far away and how all his longings lie open before the Father.

Interestingly, the study of psychology and brain science reveals that whether we identify our deepest desires or not, those core desires will motivate our decisions and the course of life we pursue. The Bible tells us what a man thinks in his heart is what makes him who he is. As every one of us discovers during life, true wholeness and fulfillment cannot be reasoned into being or simply "found" in the typical pursuits of life. That elusive happiness and completion we are all seeking after are a façade that masks the deeper longings of every human heart.

Even our greatest human joys and achievements, though great gifts, are only signposts of this more profound invitation. At their core, these longings to belong, be whole and at peace, be fulfilled, love, and find joy are invitations into a relationship with God. We were designed to be fulfilled when those core desires are met in a relationship with Him. Only then will our hearts be truly satisfied.

For followers of Jesus, this idea of fulfillment in God can still feel elusive. Without realizing it, we often pursue our desire's fulfillment in earthly things and relationships apart from God. When we do not see all as a gift and Him as the Giver, the gift becomes an idol. Again, we find ourselves wandering and wondering what has gone wrong.

As we mature and let the Holy Spirit search us, the longings of our hearts are purified and reordered. This is a lifelong process, led gently and patiently by our good Father. And whenever we find that once again, we feel the haunting ache of imperfection, perhaps we will learn to view it as a simple reminder that we are not yet Home.

You perceive my thoughts from afar.

Psalm 139:2b (NIV)

You know when I sit and when I rise;

you perceive my thoughts from afar.

You discern my going out and my lying down;

you are familiar with all my ways.

Psalm 139:2-3 NIV

Sacred or Secular

You know when I sit and when I rise;
you perceive my thoughts from afar.
You discern my going out and my lying down;
you are familiar with all my ways.

Psalm 139:2-3 (NIV)

We separate life between sacred and secular in our western culture. From viewing missions as spiritual work and corporate as a secular realm to the separation of soul and science in health care, we divide things neatly down the middle. Not so the Biblical framework and worldview. The Scriptural culture views all of life as a sacred space where God invites us to live and work with Him and let Him dwell and work in us.

This holistic view erases the hierarchy that makes one gifting or calling more important or impactful than another. Farming and missional agriculture both become a sacred way of partnering with God to manage the earth and feed people. Chaplaincy and nursing take on the same spiritual importance as people are viewed as a whole person, not just a body or just a soul. Pastoring and teaching in public schools can both be viewed as equal opportunities to proclaim love and teach wisdom. Social work and counseling become mutually part of our journey toward God and an invitation to heal our community, instead of just the solving of social and relational problems.

Viewing life this way, we can begin to walk into each moment with eyes open to see God at work in our daily lives. In our pleasure and pain, jobs and play, sabbath and travel, fellowship and friendship, food and fun, we begin to ask ourselves how we can do ALL that we do for the glory of God. It erases the myth of Sunday Christian life and involves all of us in His invitation to abundant life.

Safe

You discern my going out and my lying down...
Psalm 139:3a (NIV)

We have all experienced what it feels like to start awake to strange sounds at night. This is especially true when we are away from home or sleeping in a strange place. Sleep and travel are two of the most vulnerable states of being. Today, we may not view them quite as drastically as the Psalmist did in his day, but most children pass through a period when they are frightened of the dark. They seem to inherently realize the vulnerability that comes with the dark when most of us close our eyes to the world around us in sleep. Crime and evil often take place under cover of darkness. But the night is also a gift, and rest is as needful as air for our wellbeing. The Psalmist expressed both a knowledge of his vulnerability and a realization of where His safety came from when he wrote, "I lay down and slept, yet I woke up in safety, for the LORD was watching over me. (Psalm 3:5 NLT) and "He who watches over you will not slumber; indeed, he who watches over Israel will neither slumber nor sleep."
(Psalm 121:3b-4 NIV) When we feel safe in our surroundings, we rest easily.

Travel increases our awareness of our own vulnerability. The odds of something going wrong as we navigate the unfamiliar increase drastically. During my international travels,

I've had things stolen and lost, experienced medical emergencies in strange places, and felt the disorientation that comes from everything being different.

In the Psalmist's day, travel was notoriously dangerous. Bandits and wild animals made traveling in groups essential for safety. After his observation about the God who never sleeps, David finishes his beautiful piece of poetry with an assertion of God's care in all our comings and goings, whether day or night. "The Lord watches over you—the Lord is your shade at your right hand; the sun will not harm you by day, nor the moon by night. The Lord will keep you from all harm—He will watch over your life; the Lord will watch over your coming and going both now and forevermore." (121:5-8 NIV)

The world is not always a safe place for us. Everyone faces dangers in life. But in Him, we can find safety as we rest in the knowledge that He is with us, no matter what we face or where we go.

"Let the beloved of the Lord rest secure in Him, for He shields Him all day long, and the one the Lord loves rests between His shoulders." (Duet. 33:12b)

18

You discern my going out
and my lying down;

Psalm 139:3a (NIV)

The Blessing of Presence

You hem me in behind and before, and you lay your hand upon me.
Psalm 139:5 (NIV)

I recently took a deep dive into the Greek meaning of the word "grace." In essence grace means, "the blessing of God's presence as He leans toward us with delight." I came away with a deeper understanding of His heart for relationship with us and a fuller appreciation of His blessing.

So often, when we face life's suffering and challenges, it is easy to question whether God is really with us or if His heart is for us. In the Old Testament, the people of Israel were blessed and marked by God's presence which was expressed in tangible ways. Compared to the nations around them, they flourished. Good crops, health, an acquisition of wealth and safety, but even more markedly, God's presence was defined by access to Himself through the priests, the tabernacle, and the system of sacrifice; the Old Covenant.

Today we know this blessing differently in the New Covenant. God is still actively caring for the just and unjust alike through His created design of rhythms and seasons. But God's intimate presence is expressed to those who know Him by the indwelling of His Holy Spirit. God's grace was embodied and fulfilled by the coming of Jesus, the person of all grace and truth.

Jesus' death and resurrection closed the gap between sin-separated man—destined for death—and righteous Father, the giver of eternal life.

Another translation describes grace as God's "unfailing love and faithfulness,' and in his gospel, John captures the essence of grace expressed through Jesus as the presence of God's person when he writes:

> "The Word became flesh and made His dwelling among us. We have seen His glory, the glory of the one and only Son, who is Himself God and is at the Father's side, has made Him known." (John 14, 16-18 BSB)

Jesus' final words to His disciples before leaving for His Father were that He would be with them to the very end of this age. Through Jesus, we know grace as an invitation to relationship. Through His Spirit and His promised soon return, we know the mark of God's blessing in His living presence and an eternal future with Him.

21

Such knowledge is
too wonderful for me,
too lofty for me to attain.

Psalm 139:6 NIV

Wonder as Worship

**Such knowledge is too wonderful for me,
too lofty for me to attain.**
Psalm 139:6 (NIV)

In a heart brought into the Presence of God, wonder produces worship. The radiance of a sunset, the tenderness of a Daddy with his newborn, the shadowed quiet of twilight and dawn, the infinite vastness of the milky way spilling over the curtain of Heaven, the pounding surf of an ocean storm, the symphony of birdsong on a summer morning. All of creation worships. And in its beauty, even when we do not know Him, we sense the Presence of someone more significant, and we wonder.

This wonder goes beyond words and beyond human comprehension. This LOVE, in its vastness, is too high and long and wide and deep for us to fully KNOW this side of heaven. In Paul's words, it is a love that "Surpasses knowledge." The only way it can fully be absorbed is in lived experience and relationship with Jesus. In Heaven, we will know as we are known. Until then, such love remains a mystery, revealed in Jesus and yet, beyond us. As I meditate on the love of God, my heart swells with gratitude and praise, and I am stilled to KNOW that He is God.

Prodigal

Where can I go from your Spirit?
Where can I flee from your presence?

Psalm 139:7 (NIV)

The word prodigal is rooted in the age-old parable. A father and two sons: One who spends his Father's fortune on wanton living, far from the family home. The other brother, who slaves for his Father's approval, never realizing that all the time, the inheritance and the relationship are his for the asking. And the Father, who seeks both.

No doubt snapshots of memory come to mind for each of us when we think of the word prodigal. A teenager screaming at police and parents, her terror concealed by contempt and anger. A boy, turning man, run away from home and reported as "missing" by a worried mother. A single mom, giving birth alone, not yet entirely out of childhood herself. Someone climbing the corporate ladder, seeking the god of money instead of the God who provides. An addict in a back alley, dirty needles strewn everywhere. Regardless of the picture we conjure up in our minds, we are all prodigals. We have all strayed from our good Shepherd. And no matter how far we have run or how close to the home of religion and good works we have stayed, He invites us with the same welcoming, Fatherly love. "Come home with Me and celebrate." There is nowhere we can go that His presence will not seek and find to save, even to the uttermost parts of the earth. This is the love the Father has lavished on us, that we should be called His children.

Where can I go from your Spirit?

Where can I flee from your presence?

Psalm 139:7 (NIV)

Repentance

See if there is any offensive way in me...
Psalm 139:24a (NIV)

Repentance, as I first understood it as a child, was to list my sins to God and apologize for them. I smile now, remembering and realizing that despite His value of confession as a part of repentance, God has a slightly different view of repentance's true definition and intention than just making a laundry list of sins and saying sorry.

To repent means to turn from something else to God. It means to agree with God about truth in place of lies, and allow His Holy Spirit to cleanse us of sin and align us with Him, empowering us to live in true righteousness flowing from a transformed heart.

In the words of David's prayer, we see Him inviting God to search His heart, to look into His inner thoughts and motives, and see if there is anything that God finds offensive. So often, I define sin for myself and then tell God I don't want it in my life because I know He doesn't like it. But more and more, I realize that it's often things I'd never think of or see that are offensive to God, and that's why it's so important to invite God's Holy Spirit to search us.

When God calls me to repentance these days, it's almost always things that block or harm my relationship with Him or others that are His concern. Rarely does it have anything to do with rules or outward form. Man looks at appearances, but God searches our hearts. Whether it's self-effort toward holiness, my compliance to please others, my less than pure motivation for giving to another, or my desire for comfort that is met in something or someone other than Himself; the invitation to repentance is always an invitation back to God. Back into His loving embrace, His goodness, and His transforming power.

And as I turn and take His hand, I find the strength to let go of what I thought was good in exchange for His righteousness. To repent, in its beautiful simplicity, is to turn back toward God at His invitation and open our hands and hearts to His cleansing, transforming love.

Encompassed

Coming and going,
Daylight and dark,
Sleeping and waking,
You know every part.

Wings of the morning,
Far side of the sea,
Earth and the heavens,
Naught hides me from Thee.

In the beginning,
Formed in the womb;
And at the end,
Ashes, dust, and the tomb.

All of my moments,
All of my days,
All of my thoughts,
And all of my ways.

Always encompassed,
Behind and before,
Always beloved,
With Heaven in store.

By the Farthest Sea

**If I settle by the farthest sea,
even there Your hand will guide me;**
Psalm 139:9b-10a (BSB)

The wind blew against our faces, cool and wet with the spray of the sea. A friend and I were taking a boat from a European island where we'd served in a refugee camp for several months to the Middle East, where we'd be moving shortly. We both marveled at the peace that welled up in us. With all the unknowns before us and all the difficulty behind us, we had no idea that what lay in store in the coming years would be far more challenging.

In the weeks and months that followed, we visited a war zone and saw bombs fall. We survived a bus accident resulting in bruises and head trauma. We flew to the other side of the world to pack our things and say goodbye to our families for a longer stretch of service. And upon returning to the Middle East, we rented a tidy little apartment with a splendid rose garden and lemon trees, enclosed in a crumbling yellow plaster wall with a little white gate.

We put down roots yet constantly struggled to translate foreign ideas or customs into something relatable. We learned to shop in the market and sing hymns in a foreign language. We learned how to create new foods with foreign ingredients and walk and use public transport instead of driving our own cars. In the passing of months, we made dozens of new friends yet missed our families like crazy.

In our village by the sea, we prayed and ate, slept and woke, told stories haltingly, and listened harder. We laughed with our neighbors and cried behind closed doors. And through all the achingly beautiful days, His hand guided us, just as He'd promised.

When the day came to pack our apartment and move on into a new season of life, I grieved. I grieved leaving my home by the sea, and the losses that living there had incurred. I rejoiced at the things God had done and celebrated the relationships that had flourished. I tucked memories into my heart, even as I gave belongings away. I loved these people, even as I said goodbye. As my plane took off, the water stretching below me, I remembered His faithfulness to us, even by the farthest sea.

If I settle by the farthest sea,
even there Your hand will guide me;

Psalm 139:9b -10a (BSB)

Pursuit

Where can I flee when heaven will not hide me?
Where can I go when depths will swallow not?
This strong pursuit the knowing of all living.
That God is here, and love is stronger yet.

He knows it all, and still, He is beside me.
Offers to make His home within my humble clay.
Would I yet choose to stubbornly resist Him?
This God who knows my every way?

Ah, but this Presence is not darkness!
This Presence is the Life and Light, Divine!
Why should I flee such love and faithful kindness?
When He invites, "Beloved, come, be Mine."

Nay! Welcome in! Come search and know my being.
Come fill with love, this futile, empty shell,
And breathing love and living transformation,
In being found by you, all will be well.

When Life Feels Dark

It's impossible to disappear from you...
for your presence is everywhere, bringing light into my night.
Psalm 139:11 (TPT)

Sometimes in life we feel lost. Things get dark, and the light and certainty we once knew fades. This darkness comes in a myriad of ways: suffering, sudden loss, chronic pain, depression, a season of spiritual dryness, an unanswered prayer. Whatever our darkness, the pain is most often felt in respect to where God is in our darkness. It is easy to feel abandoned by the Father we thought was kind. We wonder why He leaves us in pain, or why He seems silent to our hearts when they most ache for His voice. We cry out in confusion and fear, like a child lost from it's parent. Or perhaps we hide in our desolation, isolating in sadness and discouragement. Has God left us behind? Do we still have His blessing on our lives?

The scripture is filled with descriptions of these times of darkness that reassure us that this too is a part of the human experience. It is filled with promises that in all of our humanity God is with us. The instructions in Scripture for these times of darkness urge us to be real with God in the process of reaching for Him in the midst of our pain. The prayers of the Psalmist ask similar questions modeling for us a pattern of lament and honesty.

"Where are you, God? How long till you come and help me? Why have you forsaken me? Come quick before I give up and die."

As frequently as he cries out with questions, the Psalmist also remembers who God is. He reminds us of God's presence and faithfulness, even when life gets dark and we don't feel God close to us. In His description of God in the darkness in Psalm 18, the author describes darkness as God's hiding place as He prepares to bring rescue to those He loves. Even when we can't see Him God is there. And when the time is right, He comes to the rescue, illuminating the darkness with brilliant light.

God knows better than anyone how much we long for the reassurance that He is with us and that He sees us, especially in the dark times. Jesus is this ultimate reassurance. By faith, we look to Him, trusting that the Promiser is true, even in the dark, because Jesus, too, experienced this darkness and overcame it for us. In His humanity He came face to face with desolation and the sense of being forsaken. On the cross He cried, "My God, My God, why have you forsaken me?" It was in this deepest darkness that He bridged the gap and made the way back to God possible for us. In His resurrection, He conquered that separation for good.

In our darkness God invites us to trust and faithfulness. Looking to Jesus, the Author and Finisher of our faith, we turn in our times of desolation to the promise that He will never leave us or forsake us, and wait for the light we know will come.

For You formed my inmost being:

You knit me together
in my mother's womb.
My frame was not hidden from You
when I was made in secret,
when I was woven together
in the depths of the earth.
Your eyes saw my unformed body...

Psalm 139:13, 15, 16a (BSB)

Womb Woven

Two become one,
Cells fusing,
Zygote.

Intricate Design Implanting,
Womb Woven,
Embryo.

Twenty-Two days,
Life flutter,
Heartbeat.

Tree of life,
New Organ,
Placenta.

Made in secret,
Gender reveal,
Ultrasound.

Light and Dark,
Mother's voice,
Rejoice!

Brain and nerves,
Week 33,
Formed.

Breath of life,
Baby cries,
Birth.

Precious

Before a word is on my tongue, you know it,
Before my birth, you'd written every day,
Lord, this is knowledge that is far beyond me;
A mystery of love, what can I say?

Bound by that cord of making in Your image,
Your thoughts toward me as numberless as sand,
How precious this, Your thoughts toward me as Father,
My inward parts, created by Your Hand.

First cry, first breath, a miracle of being!
Brought forth to know and to make known this love.
Fearful and wonderful, a child, say Gloria Deo!
A mirroring of salvation's birth above.

All My Days

All the days ordained for me...
Psalm 139:16 (NIV)

I sit in the morning sunlight and watch the two of them, my grandmother and my niece, at the breakfast table. Lulu picks at her breakfast cereal, her rogue blond hair sticking in every direction. She turns large inquisitive blue eyes on her great-grandmother. "Hi!" she says, grinning enthusiastically. "Hi! Yea! Yea!" She giggles as if she has told the biggest joke and hides her face in her hands.

Grandma watches her with a mixture of bemusement and perplexity. Her childhood was in an era of children seen and not heard. The years since her own children were small stretch far behind, and her age is reflected in her thin, lined face. When Lulu says hi for the sixteenth time in a row, Grandma says, "I don't know what that's all about."

I smile. "It's all she knows how to say. She's just practicing her words." Lulu is not quite two. Grandma nods and lifts her teacup, her hands blue-veined and frail but still reminiscent of the refinement of her youth. This is how the conversation unfolds each Friday when Lulu comes to visit me, where I live and care for my grandmother. And in the love and perplexity with which these two regard each other, I see a reflection of God's promise that He is with us all our days.

From the first tiny developing cell in our mother's womb to the tottering steps of old age, from the first stumbling words as a lisping toddler to the words we forget when our minds grow tired. Every day. Every season. Babe, child, youth. Adult, parent, elderly. All these days are ordained by Him. All our days, He is with us.

All the days ordained for me...

Psalm 139:16 (NIV)

In Your Book

**All the days ordained for me were written
in your book before one of them came to be.**

Psalm 139:16b (NIV)

I am a planner by nature. I love to think and process ahead, make lists, and finish projects before their deadlines. But for all my careful planning, I am far enough into life to realize that things rarely go as planned. When life goes off the rails, it is easy to wonder if God has a plan for our life. Are we just wandering aimlessly in a world of chance, or does God design and number our days?

In the Psalmist's view, God had ordained each of his days. He had planned each of those days with care. In fact, He had written down each of them in His book before one of these days ever happened.

As the author of over a dozen books, this image captures me. A book has a beginning, an order, a clear progression, and an ending. It makes me think of the Hebrews writer who called Jesus the "Author and Finisher of our faith."

Early in my faith walk, I thought very concretely about God's intended plans for me. I saw His direction in going to specific places and doing particular things as I served Him. I saw life as linear more than cyclical, and spiritual growth as something to practice and pursue.

As I mature, I am catching a more profound vision of God's plan. Often there are elements of my daily life that He does direct or ordain. I do not doubt that He takes an interest in the details of my life, just as a parent does their child. But as the Author and Finisher of my faith, the bigger plan, the deeper realization, is that God's desire and invitation in all my days, plans, years, and life is to walk in a loving relationship and partnership with Him. To grow and mature into being like Him by being with Him. As I learn to walk shoulder to shoulder, moment by moment, with a good God in kingdom partnership, I grow spiritually. And as I grow up into the love of God, I realize that it is not so much my doing in my days that is His primary plan of focus, but my becoming. By becoming unified with His heart, in love, and embodying that love to others.

*I can never escape
from your Spirit!*

**I can never get away from your presence!
(even) if I ride the wings
of the morning.**

Psalm 139:7, 9a (NLT)

Wings of Morning — Speed of Light

I can never escape from your Spirit!
I can never get away from your presence!
(Even) if I ride the wings of the morning.
Psalm 139:7,9a (NLT)

Sunrise. Glory of light after darkness. A glimmer of prism in spider's orbs and grasses touched with dew drops. A golden wash of newness breaking everywhere. Anywhere, over an ocean, a cityscape, or through the deeper shadows of forest and mountain crags, sunrise is welcome. Daily it comes, a herald of new mercy. Consistent, unchanging. Steady. And in that light, we see reflections of His light. Illuminating His faithfulness.

"Wings of the morning," the Psalmist called it. In Psalm 139's extensive catalog of God's reach, we hear the declaration that wherever we are, we cannot escape and are never lost to God's all-knowing kindness. Even if we were to harness the fastest thing in the universe, the speed of light, this would not be fast enough to take us outside the ever-present goodness of our Creator. Paul's much later epistles would reiterate this same truth, declaring that nothing could separate God's children from His love," nothing in all creation." In 2 Corinthians 4:6 (BSB), He illuminates the nature and revelation of the Creator of light and knowing, "For God, who said, "Let light shine out of darkness," made his light shine in our hearts to give us the light of the knowledge of the glory of God in the face of Christ." To know Christ is the ultimate fulfillment of all-knowing. To enter in as the beloved.

Morning Glory

Dawn,
Sun rising,
Gold tinged East.
Darkness dissipates,
Dispelling shadows.
Light touches dew.
Shimmering,
Shining,
The whole morning fills,
The glory of new mercies.

If I fly with wings into the shining dawn, you're there!

Psalm 139:9 (TPT)

Thoughts as Sand

How precious are your thoughts about me, O God. They cannot be numbered! I can't even count them; they outnumber the grains of sand!
Psalm 139:17-18a (NLT)

In his sweeping imagery, the Psalmist compares God's thoughts toward us as more than the sand by the sea. This picture has always captured me. Whenever I visit the ocean or spend time on a beach, I ponder with wonder the intensely tiny yet numberless grains of sand under my feet. A Google search will reveal that in all the beaches and deserts on our planet, there are approximately seven quintillion, five hundred quadrillion grains of sand. That is a lot of thoughts!

But God does not simply think about us in passing or as objects. He thinks about us in a profoundly personal way. Even more boggling than the sheer quantity of sand is the fact that every grain of sand in the world is unique, just like snowflakes or fingerprints—no two alike, unique and beautiful under a microscope. So too, God's thoughts toward us are individual, beautifully unique, and deeply personal.

Scripture assures us that He knows us by name and records all our days in His book. Just as he calls the stars forth by name, which outnumber sand by an estimated 10,000 to 1 in number, He calls each person created in His image by name. Awe-inspiring! Too vast to truly grasp or comprehend and yet, so near and intimate that He calls us, you and me, by name. What an intimate knowing! What an abundant love!

When I awake, I am still with you.

Psalm 139:18b (NIV)

New Every Morning

When I awake, I am still with you.
Psalm 139:18b (NIV)

This morning as I looked out at the giant oak that shades my balcony, waiting for the coffee to brew, I listened to the morning bird symphony and pondered with deep joy that every day I get to meet Jesus in a fresh way. Not everyone is a morning person, but for me, that early quiet, with coffee and a pen poised over my journal to record what He wants to speak to me through His Word, is something I treasure.

This practice for me was born from watching the faithfulness of my earthly parent. Growing up, I could count on my mom to be there when I woke up, early in the morning, her Bible in front of her, journaling what Jesus was teaching. Year in and year out, morning by morning, this lived example forged in me a joyous understanding of faithful relationship and investment. It is one of the rituals of my relationship with Jesus that I rarely skip. When I stop to realize what this consistency brings in building the intimacy and trust between my heart and Jesus, I am reminded of His character.

Like I count on our time in the early morning quiet, with a rich, steaming cup of coffee and the written word of Scripture to nourish my soul, I also count on His new mercies to be faithful for each new day that comes. As the writer of Lamentations profoundly summarizes, "The steadfast love of the Lord never ceases; His mercies never come to an end; they are new every morning; great is Your faithfulness." (3:22-23 ESV) We need not doubt such enduring love. Jesus said that sufficient unto each day would be its trouble. But overarching and undergirding this reality is the bedrock truth that God, in His kindness, is faithful. With seasons and sunrise, day and night, we see the ritual faithfulness of His steady love. We do not need to worry when we sleep at night that tomorrow may be different or absent of His presence. He has already gone ahead of us into tomorrow. He is with us while we sleep. And in waking to each new morning, we will find that the God of mercy is still with us. And for this day, as for yesterday, and again tomorrow, His mercies for us are new.

Search me, God, and know my heart...

Psalm 139:23a (NIV)

Invitation

Search me, God, and know my heart...
Psalm 139:23a (NIV)

As the beautiful words of Psalm 139 come to a close, we see the poet's focus shift from God's giving to his own response. All throughout, he has been exploring how God pursues, knows, and loves us. As the Psalm ends, we see his desire to open his heart to God in return.

David declares his loyalty to God and invites God to intimately know his heart and thoughts. He asks God to remove anything that might come in the way of their intimacy. He speaks of this same shared friendship between God and His people in Psalm 25:14. (NLT) "The LORD confides in those who fear Him and reveals His covenant to them."

For those who know they are loved by God, the natural response to the awe-inducing wonder of His devoted love and faithfulness is to seek to love Him in return. From Genesis and the garden of Eden, where man walked and talked with God in the cool of the day, to the Revelation, where Jesus is united to His people as His bride at His return, we see the story and the invitation to intimacy etched in the pages of Scripture. It is the very essence of God's design, to know and be known and to be completed in love.

53

Transforming Peace

Test me and know my anxious thoughts.
Psalm 139:23b NIV

Some of my favorite verses are found in the Gospel of John, just before Jesus goes to the cross. Being troubled by the great weight of suffering He would bear in the following hours, He sought to prepare His disciples for the perplexity and suffering they, too, were about to face. "I am leaving you with a gift—peace of mind and heart. And the peace I give is a gift the world cannot give... So don't be troubled or afraid. I have told you all this so that you may have peace in me. Here on earth, you will have many trials and sorrows. But take heart because I have overcome the world." John 14:27 and John 16:33 NLT

Our natural human tendency during trouble is to worry. To become anxious and fearful or to try and solve the problems we are facing and escape the suffering they bring. Jesus invites us to another way. Paul outlines this way and its transformative effects in Philippians 4:6-7 NIV "Do not be anxious about anything, but in every situation, by prayer and petition, with thanksgiving, present your requests to God. And the peace of God, which transcends all understanding, will guard your hearts and your minds in Christ Jesus."

Jesus invites us to find peace in His person. In remembering the power and goodness of the God who is carefully and attentively looking after each of His children. In every moment of our lives, as we bring our problems to Him, big or small, we receive and embrace God's healing comfort and protective provision. Amid the imperfections and perplexities of our days, we begin to understand His goodness, and our trust deepens.

Sometimes He changes the things we face, and sometimes He does not. But as we know Him, whether in the relief of our suffering or in the fellowship of His presence in our suffering, we begin to be transformed by a heavenly perspective. In place of anxiety, Jesus begins to bring deep peace and wholeness that is born from knowing our completion in Christ. His presence gives us rest. His grace becomes sufficient. And as we run with patience and endure, we do so with our eyes on the One who has gone before us, knowing one day He will end all suffering and set all things right. With His encouraging voice in our ears, we lean on His kind strength and trust Him, knowing that soon, He will come, and all will be well. And on that day, we who shared His suffering will also share His glory

Test me and know my anxious thoughts...

Psalm 139:23b (NIV)

And lead me in the way everlasting.

Psalm 139:24b (NIV)

Revelation

And lead me in the way everlasting.
Psalm 139:24b (NIV)

The theme of everlasting or eternal life is woven all through the Bible. It is the gift of God to those who believe in the promise of Heaven and Christ's return, making all things new.

For many, Heaven is a faraway concept. Some have adopted the typical "harp and cloud" picture or a haunting sense of boredom over the idea of an eternal worship service. But what if our misconceptions of Heaven do a profound injustice to God's promise of eternal life? What if we were made for so much more than an eternally dull church service in the clouds? Perhaps this nagging uncertainty can spur us on to a higher vision instead of guilt.

In his classic book called "Heaven," Randy Alcorn leads readers in a deep and detailed exploration of the wonder, beauty, and delight of what Everlasting life with Jesus will be like according to Scripture. Revelation is full of descriptions of beautiful architecture, sweeping landscapes, and nature in all its healing beauty. It speaks of restored wholeness of relationships in humanity and the incredible and wonderful fulfillment of knowing Jesus fully and in person. Now we see through a glass darkly, but then we will see Him face to face.

"And I heard a loud voice from the throne saying, "Look! God's dwelling place is now among the people, and He will dwell with them. They will be His people, and God Himself will be with them and be their God. 'He will wipe every tear from their eyes. There will be no more death' or mourning or crying or pain, for the old order of things has passed away." He who was seated on the throne said, "I am making everything new!" Then he said, "Write this down, for these words are trustworthy and true." Revelations 21:3-5 (NIV)

In the new heaven and earth, meaningful creative work, joy, laughter, feasting, dwelling, and togetherness will be at their eternal best. All things will be restored to their fullest glory, without any shadow of pain, tears, or suffering left to mar the scene. And we shall be forever with the Lord.

Acknowledgments

Author: This book would not have been possible without a creative community's joyful collaboration. It was a book project born of a desire to ponder wonder as worship of our good and loving Creator, and the artists who invested many hours of shared and individual creative input were the ones who made the dream a reality.

Thank you, Mom, for the hours spent by the river in the castle house painting, writing, reading, and discussing this book. Thank you for pouring your whole soul into your beautiful paintings. Thanks for breathing color and texture into every page of this shared worship endeavor. With you, I felt His pleasure. With you, I rejoice at a finished work.

Thank you, Tracia. As our graphic designer, your skilled, generous, and beautiful work took our loose-leaf pages and turned them into a cohesive and stunning whole. Thank you for sharing your gifts in this work. Creating with you has been a sheer pleasure.

Thank you, Anna and Given, for believing in the power of words and giving much-valued feedback on content edits, publishing options, and theological perspectives. Your input gave me the confidence to finish this work, just as your friendship gives me confidence in life's goodness.

Artist: Thanks to our wonderful LORD Jesus for knowing me intimately and loving me abundantly. I'm forever grateful for His inspiration of the Psalmist whose words penned so long ago still touch my heart every time I read them. And for His blessing my daughter Rachael with words as she wrote celebrating this knowledge and love.

I'm indebted to my parents, David and Barbara Smith, both now knowing fully as they are known, in Heaven, for always encouraging my art. I remember my Dad giving me art supplies and materials from a young age, and when I took up watercolor painting as an adult he learned alongside me, spending his Saturdays painting with me. He sent my paintings to a man from his church who matted and framed them, believing as only a parent could that they were good enough to be framed. My mom encouraged me by admiring my paintings and hanging any I gave her.

Thank you, Rachael, you inspire me spiritually with your intimate relationship with our Jesus. I love your ability to express ideas in beautiful moving words. I can't express enough the joy it was to work together on this project - it was a sheer act of worship! Thank you for including me.

Artist Biographies

Rachael and Patti Lofgren

Author: As a communicator and storyteller, Rachael seeks to see God's bigger story woven through people's everyday lives. The author of numerous published biographical and historical works with a background in communications, international humanitarian aid, and spiritual formation through Spiritual Direction, her passion is to champion personal discipleship, healing, community, and maturity in the body of Christ among the nations. Nourishing others in their relationship with Christ and their understanding of His love brings her joy.

Artist: As an artist, Patti enjoys working in various mediums, including watercolor and oil paint. Passionate about art and education for the glory of God, along with homeschooling, she enjoys sharing art experiences with her children and grandchildren. She sees the beauty in the world as God's canvas of love, and for her, art is both a form of communal pleasure and of worship.

This artistic mother-daughter duo delights in working together to produce material that inspires others to understand God's love personally and worship Him more fully through their combination of art and words.

Tracia Ropp

Graphic Designer: Tracia's love for typography, layout, and all things Indesign is fueled by a passion for the Creator and the way He creates. She also finds few things as thrilling as watching His masterpieces living in their unique God-given identity, and loves the synergy that happens when these individuals come together to collaborate as agents of goodness, beauty, and light in the midst of a pain-filled, broken, dark world.